D0375991

# The Little Book of

Tea

# The Little Book of

# Tea

## RANDY BURGESS

*Ariel Books*

**Andrews McMeel
Publishing**

Kansas City

Library of Congress Catalog Card Number: 97-74530

Copyright © 1998 by Armand Eisen. All rights reserved.
Printed in Hong Kong. No part of this book may be
used or reproduced in any manner whatsoever without
written permission except in the case of reprints in
the context of reviews. For information write Andrews McMeel Publishing, an Andrews McMeel
Universal company, 4520 Main Street,
Kansas City, Missouri 64111.

www.andrewsmcmeel.com
ISBN: 0-8362-5227-6

# CONTENTS

TEA brings a universal smile. It is warm, understood in virtually every language, and welcome around the globe. The drink brewed from the leaf of *Camellia sinensis* is consumed with equal cheer by nomads in the Himalayas and sheepherders in Australia, Russian apparatchiks and British lorry drivers, and even Americans

lucky enough to be acquainted with its charms.

But tea has also caused great trouble. British greed for the beverage led to the Opium Wars between Britain and China in the nineteenth century; a tax on tea symbolized British tyranny to the American colonies and led to the Boston Tea Party of 1773.

But let's leave politics aside. How do you like your tea—with milk to soothe, or lemon for bite? Should it be a black, full-bodied Assam from northeastern India? A ruby-colored Darjeeling, fragrant as muscatel? Or a green tea, such as a

pale, pleasingly bitter Gunpowder?

Whether tea is a new acquaintance or an old friend, you'll find the story behind it full of surprises. Read on for a taste of the lore—at once earthy and heavenly—that infuses every cup, whether brewed from the freshest blossom or the bitterest dregs. Stage a little tea party of your own.

# A POTFUL OF
# TEA TRIVIA

$\mathcal{I}$s tea good or bad for you? A little of both. Green tea not only contains vitamin C, but also inhibits the formation of cancer-causing substances called nitrosamines in the body. Tea of all kinds has been shown to help reduce cholesterol. On the negative side, tea contains caffeine, and too much caffeine is blamed for insomnia and other ills.

*H*erbal teas are not, properly speaking, tea at all, but infusions of various plants generally considered medicinal in folklore. Tea from valerian root has been proven to aid sleep, tea from peppermint soothes the stomach, and tea from chamomile flowers combines both virtues.

*O*ne of the many enticing mysteries of Russian literature is the samovar, which shows up in novels by Tolstoy and short stories by Chekhov. This is a combined teakettle and teapot. It consists of a metal urn, with a top section for brewing a concentrated batch of tea, a bottom section from which you can draw hot water to dilute your tea to taste, and a chimney to hold charcoal and keep everything hot. Tea brewed this way was so strong that devotees drank it through a sugar cube held between their teeth.

The tea bag was invented accidentally in 1908 by Thomas Sullivan, a New York importer. Sullivan was sending out samples of different kinds of

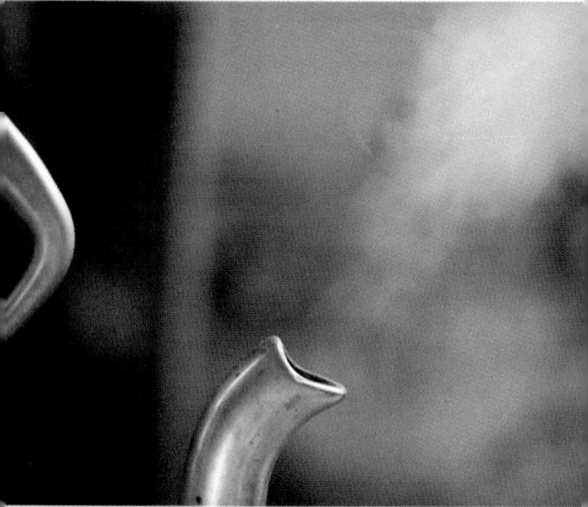

tea in little silk bags; a customer dunked a bag and found it marvelously convenient.

When preparing most kinds of tea, you should bring the water to a rolling boil before pouring it into the teapot; the air in the boiling water helps unfold the leaves. Green tea, however, should be made with water just short of full boil. And don't use a metal tea ball: It confines the tea leaves too much, preventing them from becoming fully suffused.

Afternoon tea, that British institution, was invented by Anna, the seventh

Duchess of Bedford. In the late 1700s the aristocracy ate large breakfasts, larger dinners in the evening, and not much in between. To get around what she described as a mid-afternoon "sinking feeling," the duchess began the practice of ordering tea and cakes. Soon her friends were staving off their own sinking feelings in the same manner.

Tea first made its way to Russia on the backs of camels. Beginning in the late seventeenth century, caravans started south from Moscow with furs to trade, and came back with crates of tea. Each round-

trip took nearly a year. Russians drank their tea out of glasses, not cups, because Chinese porcelain was too bulky and fragile to be carried by the caravans.

The Chinese were so secretive about the tea they exported that at first, the English believed black and green tea came from two different species of plant. Finally, in 1848, the British East India Company sent a Scottish botanist named Robert Fortune to China. Disguising himself as a Chinese, Fortune discovered that tea was tea; the only difference was in the processing.

*I*ced tea was invented at the St. Louis World's Fair in 1904. The summer heat was so scorching that no one would drink  the hot tea being promoted by British tea merchants until one of them, Richard Blechynden, hit upon the idea of pouring the tea over ice.

TEA

OVER TIME

## All the Tea in China

The origin of tea isn't history but legend. Its hero is Shen Nong, a revered Chinese emperor who lived three thousand years before the birth of Christ. In his sagacity, Shen Nong taught his people to boil water, to make it safely drinkable. He himself was doing so one day, out of doors, when a few leaves fell into the bowl from a bush that we now know as *Camellia sinensis*. The emperor tasted the resulting infusion—and pronounced it medicine, but medicine that tasted good.

Many centuries later tea had asserted itself as a part of everyday Chinese life. In the fifth century A.D., a poet of the Jin dynasty wrote that the taste for fragrant tea had spread over the nine districts—in other words, throughout all of China.

## Tea Takes over Japan

In A.D. 805, a Japanese monk named Dengyo Daishi returned from China to his native land, bringing with him seeds of the tea plant. So impressed were the Japanese by this new drink that they invented yet another legend to account for its origin.

In the Japanese version, the Indian monk Daruma vowed to meditate for nine straight years without sleeping. Five years into the ordeal, he began to nod off, to his dismay. Cutting

off his eyelids to prevent future catnaps, Daruma threw them to the ground—and a tea plant sprouted where they fell.

## Tea Arrives in Europe

In 1610, enterprising Dutch traders introduced the first few pounds of tea to Europe, importing it from Japan. By 1685, tea drinkers in Holland were consuming more than twenty thousand pounds a year. Grocers stocked it, wealthy burghers added tearooms to their houses, and matrons usurped beer halls to host tea clubs.

For some reason, tea skipped France, which favored wine, hopscotched over

Germany, which swore by beer, but landed full stop in England—an island that already had ale and coffee but apparently wasn't satisfied.

## The British Fancy

In 1670, famed diarist Samuel Pepys noted that he had experimented with a "cup of tee (a China drink) of which I never had drank before." After that, it was only a matter of time before the entire British Empire submerged itself in a teacup.

Journalist Joseph Addison advised his readers that morning tea was an essential part of "all well-regulated households."

Samuel Johnson, who authored the first dictionary of the English language, was known to drink dozens of cups a day, and once described himself as "a hardened and shameless tea-drinker, who for twenty years . . . with tea amused the evening, with tea solaced the midnight, and with tea welcomed the morning." By the late 1700s, the thirsty English were sipping their way through nearly five million tons of tea a year.

## The Opium Wars

Tea also led Britain to commit one of the most shameful acts in that country's history—the supplying of opium to China as a means of supporting the British tea habit.

By the late eighteenth century, Britain was importing so much tea from China that the cost was draining British silver reserves. The solution lay in the opium crop being grown in the British colony of India. The importation of opium was illegal in China, but the British began smuggling it in anyway. The profits paid Britain's bill for its beverage of choice.

In 1839, the frustrated Chinese government seized twenty thousand chests of British opium warehoused at the port of

Canton, and burned it on the beach. Tensions rose. The final British response was to declare war.

Britain won this First Opium War in 1842. Not only was China forced to legal-

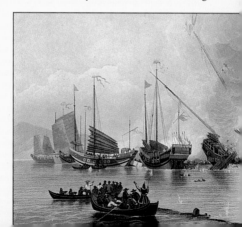

ize opium imports, it had to turn over Hong Kong to the Crown. A second Opium War occurred in 1857; the British won again and burned the emperor's summer palace to the ground. The opium

trade boomed, along with the number of addicts. It wasn't until 1908 that the drug was finally banned in China.

## America and the Clipper Ship

The first American settlers brought their tea habit with them to the New World, but their interest cooled after the Boston Tea Party, when angry colonists tossed crates of the stuff into Boston Harbor to protest unfair British taxes. The situation warmed only slightly after the Revolution, and America never did become a bastion for tea. One of our inventions did make it easier for the rest of the world, however: the

speedy clipper ship, designed to hasten the long, damp voyage from China. Among other things, this helped to keep cargoes of tea leaves from getting moldy.

In 1845 the first clipper, the *Rainbow*, made the passage from New York Harbor to China and back in less than eight months. Ships quickly became even faster after that. Once the British began building clippers, they held an annual race to deliver the first spring crop from China to the London docks. The record, eighty-nine days, was set in 1869. It still stands today.

FROM LEAF TO CUP

*F*ew of us would recognize a tea plant—*Camellia sinensis*—if we came across it. The leaves are glossy and oval; the small, white flowers are similar to apple blossoms.

The tea plant grows new leaves at least once a year. Young leaves are called a flush; much of the best tea is made from the first, tenderest flush of the spring. Equally valuable is the leaf bud at the tip of the shoot. This bud, with its covering of fine hair or down, is called the pekoe, from the Chinese *bai hao*, meaning "white hair." The more down, the better the taste of the tea.

If there is only one species of tea plant, how is it that there are so many varieties of tea?

First, just as with wine grapes, the character of the tea leaf is influenced by soil and climate. Second, there are many different subspecies, or varietals, of tea—about two thousand in all. Finally, teas differ because of how they are processed. There are three main types: black (fermented), green (unfermented), and oolong (partially fermented).

---

**BLACK TEA** is made by spreading the harvested leaves on trays, and allowing them to wither, or dry. The leaves are then rolled and crushed, allowed to ferment, and fired till dry.

---

**GREEN TEA** as enjoyed in China and Japan, is almost like drinking the leaf in its natural state. The freshly picked leaves are steamed to destroy any enzymes that might

cause fermentation, and then rolled and
fired.

❧❧❧❧❧❧❧❧

OOLONG is unusual, and not just for its
name, which is Chinese for "black dragon."
The leaves for oolong are plucked at their
peak of growth. They're wilted in sunlight,
then lightly bruised by being shaken
in bamboo baskets.

When the leaves are
only partially fer-
mented, they are
fired.

## EARL GREY

This tea derives its unmistakable flavor from the addition of bergamot—an oil from the rind of a pear-shaped citrus fruit

# WUYI OOLONG
### THE CUP OF POETRY
*Finest Formosan Silver-Tip Tea*

## The REPUBLIC of TEA

*brews 60 cups*
Full Leaf Loose Tea
NetWt 1.75 oz (50g)

# CHAMOMILE LEMON
### SURRENDER TO SLEEP HERB TEA
*Naturally Caffeine Free*

## The REPUBLIC of TEA

*brews 60 cups*
Fresh Full Leaf Herbs and Flowers
NetWt 1.75 oz (50g)

# MAN
###

## The RE

## YLON

EA

Leaves
f Fruit

# TEA OF INQUIRY

BLENDED GREEN LEAF WITH TOASTED RICE

*Finest Traditional Genmaicha*

# The REPUBLIC of TEA

brews 60 cups

*Full Leaf Loose Tea*

Net Wt 3.5 oz (100g)

# ALL DAY BREAKFAST

KEEMUN OOLONG TEA

*World's Finest Breakfast Tea Leaves*

# The REPUBLIC of TEA

brews 60 cups

*Full Leaf Loose Tea*

Net Wt 3.5 oz (100g)

that grows around the Mediterranean. It's named after Earl Charles Grey, who served as a diplomat in China in the 1830s and later became Britain's prime minister.

ENGLISH
BREAKFAST

The name of this tea is a marketing gimmick, going back over a hundred years; the name implies a nice strong tea to wake you up. Once, English Breakfast was made exclusively from *Keemun,* a strong China black tea; these days it's often a blend.

## LAPSANG SOUCHONG

This famous black tea is aggressive and pungent. Leaves are smoked over a pine fire to give it its distinctive flavor.

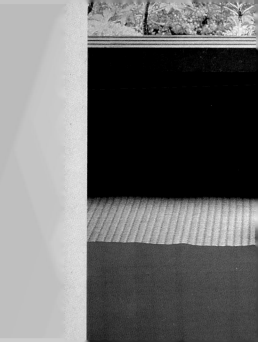

## FORMOSA OOLONG

Fruity as a ripe peach, this tea is often described as "the champagne of teas." (So is *Darjeeling*.) It is best enjoyed plain.

## JASMINE

Jasmine is green tea, perfumed with the red, yellow, or white blossoms of the jasmine plant. It is served in Chinese restaurants throughout the world. Try it weak, to tame the jasmine, and add some lemon.

## MATCHA

Matcha is the ceremonial green tea of Japan, a fine green powder, curiously rich in vitamin C. Unlike most green teas, it is sweet and smooth, never bitter.

THE LITERARY
TEA BAG

"Take some more tea," the March Hare said to Alice, very earnestly.

"I've had nothing yet," Alice replied in an offended tone: "so I can't take more."

"You mean you can't take *less*," said the Hatter: "it's very easy to take *more* than nothing."

LEWIS CARROLL

*ALICE'S ADVENTURES IN WONDERLAND*

Most people can let four o'clock pass without stopping everything (as I am still unable to—despite American citizenship and more than a quarter-century's U.S. residence).

COLIN FLETCHER
*THE COMPLETE WALKER III*,
ON AFTERNOON TEA

THE LITTLE BOOK OF TEA

My grandmother died before tea bags. I am thankful. My mother never admitted their existence. A friend has described them as boiled mice, and he is right too, but I have some teas in little white bags for people who have never known anything else, and who are adept enough to leave the wee tail hanging over the edge of the cup.

M. F. K. FISHER
INTRODUCTION TO JAMES NORWOOD
PLATT'S *THE TEA LOVER'S TREASURY*

The best quality leaves must have creases like the leathern boot of Tartar horsemen, curl like the dewlap of a mighty bullock, unfold like a mist rising out of a ravine, gleam like a lake touched by a zephyr, and be wet and soft like fine earth newly swept by rain.

LU YU
*THE CLASSIC OF TEA*

Thank God for tea! What would the world do without tea?—how did it exist? I am glad I was not born before tea.

SYDNEY SMITH
*LADY HOLLAND'S MEMOIR*

*Composed in Centaur, Shelley Allegro, and Copperplate*
*with QuarkXpress™ and Adobe® Illustrator™*
*on the Macintosh computer*

*Book design and composition by*
*Judith Stagnitto Abbate*
*of Abbate Design*

*Photographs on case and pp. 48–49 copyright © Harry*
*Smith Collection; endpapers and pp. 2,18,61 copyright ©*
*Robert Egan; pp. 6, 9,17,50, 66–67 copyright © 1998*
*Gregory K. Clark; pp. 11, 14, 20, 24, 25, 54–55, 56,*
*68, 71, 72, 76, 78–79 copyright © Koren Trygg; pp. 12–*
*13, 22, 26–27, 28, 32, 40–41 courtesy Government*
*Information Office, Republic of China; pp. 31, 33, 62–63*
*courtesy Japan National Tourist Organization; p. 34 cour-*
*tesy Lenox Brands; pp. 47, 64 copyright © Fortnum &*
*Mason; pp. 58–59 courtesy The Republic of Tea; p. 75*
*courtesy the Tea Board of India.*